A DIAMOND IS HARD BUT NOT TOUGH

by

Ann Rae Jonas

Winner of the 1997 Washington Prize

THE WORD WORKS
WASHINGTON, DC

First Edition
First Printing
A Diamond Is Hard But Not Tough

Printed in the U.S.A.
Book design, typography by: Janice Olson
Cover art: "Circle" by Randy Jewart

Library of Congress Number: 97-061463
International Standard Book Number: 0-915380-36-6

◊

ACKNOWLEDGMENTS

The following poems (or earlier versions) appeared in *Hanging Loose*: "In the Afternoon"; *Songs from Unsung Worlds: Science in Poetry* (an anthology published by Birkhäuser Boston and *Science 85*): "The Causes of Color," "The Cat in the Box"; *River City:* "Everything Moves," "Time Dilation"; *Crosscurrents; A Quarterly:* "Phantom Light"; *Frank:* "Knot Theory," "Torque"; *GW Review:* "Maps"; *Artful Dodge:* "Force Diagram," "Structures"; *Seneca Review:* "Measurement."

I thank my editor, Hilary Tham, for her insights and enthusiasm.

for my mother,
Helen Schlesinger

and my husband,
Bruce Hrnjez

◊

CONTENTS

I

II

III

IV

V

I

Force Diagram

Start with gravity.
An arrow presses down
from my head to my feet.

The Earth presses up.
Small arrows jab my feet
and follow as I walk.

Arrows press in all around,
while those beneath my skin
press out. The air
would crush me if it could.

Maps

A city is shaped like an apple,
a shoe, a bar of soap.
Walking the streets,
you struggle to reduce a world
to the map that contains it.

◊

Eskimo fishermen carve
pocketpieces of wood
in the shape of the coastline.
Out on the water, the fingers
read the familiar curves.

◊

You can draw the bed and radio
as stars or circles,
make them both the same size.

But the bed must go
under the wood-framed skylight

and the radio on the ledge,
where Bach is drowned out by
the jazz of passing trains.

◊

Draw the serpentine road,
but not the crosses
planted where people have died;

forestland, but not the tracks
on the forest floor.

◊

To map the ocean floors,
a surveyor sends a sound
below the boat
and times the echo's return.

I speak. The length of your pause
before you respond
is a measure of your depth
or inattention.

◊

To map a tract of land,
you measure then draw.

Yet no matter how small
the increments,
beginning and end
never quite meet—
the error of closure.

Did the Eskimo

who carved coastlines on small sticks of wood, turning
the corner and continuing back on the other side,
did he feel like a god picking up a tool
to prod the handiwork of time,
the eroding and folding and heaving up (that he
probably had no idea of the unfathomable slowness of),
did he sense as he followed a trail to the water's edge
or fished along the Greenland coast, his kayak
scribing its own ephemeral map on the water,
did he sense a process of making, if not a maker?

Or did the Eskimo who carved a map
think instead of the junctions and mounds
of his wife's body as she lay at night,
worn from dressing skins, from sewing and cooking,
from carrying the catch down the mountain to sell,
then standing in the store to buy hooks and twine,
to trade sallies and advice about children and home,
about a man who carried his world in his pocket,
his fingers tracing the journey just past and
the journey about to come, satisfied that they made
a compact, knowable shape?

Stroke by Stroke

Carrying food, tools, field notes, gifts of seed and iron
for Indians they met along the way; long days spent
scanning the horizon for storms, attending to hunger and
thirst, to sweat-soaked clothes and muscles growing strong;

the rhythm of rowing a background to thought, to talk of
God and how they'd save the Indians—counting paddle
strokes, the Jesuits made their way around Lake Superior
and drew a map, the finest for 150 years.

The goal was not the usual one of a journey: to cover distance
and arrive. Nor was it simply to count: sacks of provisions emptied,
paddles worn and lost. They did count strokes—work itself
was the unit of measure—but through the measured wake,
the Jesuits earned the revelation of shape.

Measurement

First we count. One cat. Ted.
Two cats. Zoe. Three cats. Myron.
Then we standardize units. How many
heads above me do you stand
(making it hard
to kiss like in the movies)?

The Inca unit of time was
how long it took to cook a potato.
Waiting for frozen broccoli to microwave,
I interrupt your reading twice
with questions that could have waited.
Two questions per box.

We measure our marriage.
How many books we've read together.
Silences divided by laughter, turned pages,
one person walking out.
We place calipers around our wrists,
houseplants, piles of unpaid bills.

The essence of infinity is that the whole
does equal a part.
If love were infinite, one kind gesture
would equal a lifetime of trust;
a single betrayal, a marriage made in hell.
One cat. Two cats. Three cats.

Cartography

...more information can be read from a map than was needed to construct it.

John Ziman, *Reliable Knowledge*

Placement is easy—
New York, Chicago and Austin
form a triangle for everyone,
Paris stays in France.

A map's legend conveys
its maker's needs and quirks.
Bookshop, fruit stand, park,
descend the white margin.

◊

This map will include the past: Lithuania,
where Grandpa was born, descended from
the Vilna Gaon, great Jewish scholar
who tried to crush the vulgar Hasidim.

Draw a long line from Vilna
to Philadelphia, where my parents attend
their Reform temple.

◊

On trips to New York, Norma and I competed
to be the first to spot "New Jersey|New York"
on the Holland Tunnel wall (being older,
I usually won). The game lost its thrill
heading back to Philadelphia.

◊

In Paris, I modeled for art classes, babysat,
typed pornography, stole Virginia Woolf's essays
from an English-language bookstore, and had
my first serious lover (from Evanston, Illinois).

In the Luxembourg Gardens, I watched
children sail toy boats on the pond. The sky
was hazy blue above delicate trees.

As children, we would retreat from anger
to basement or scant backyard.
Sundays, we were taken to the art museum,
to look at Impressionist paintings.

◊

Some places, though lacking detail,
loom larger than scale.
Bend, Oregon, where Norma lost her life.

First draw a line from O'Hare to Bend.
My father at the airport; in his overnight bag,
her dental impressions for identification.

Then the road past the field where they found her,
the tiny courthouse where we met the assistant D.A.
(but not the killer in the upstairs jail).

The motel from where I called my mother,
to say that they were certain.

◊

All the New York apartments,
each with stained refrigerator,
window frames with regenerating
mounds of dirt between window and sill,
locks on heavy doors.

The map symbol for each, a mailbox.
Depot for poetry rejections,
the occasional acceptance;
letters from a lover in Toronto,

unemployment checks,
a photo of me with my head cut off,
left by a rejected boyfriend.

CODA

Fargo and Minneapolis are snow-
covered and cold. Planes drop me mail
and the *New York Times.* I follow
the departing planes with my eyes.
They leave no trail, no map in the sky.

II

Lapidary

A gemstone bears
little glory in the rough—
it must be coaxed to catch light.
The cutter's compromise
is between beauty and size.

The Causes of Color

Natural alexandrites are very rare,
red in candlelight
blue-green in the sun.

The color is generated by
chromium ions—impurities.

Impurity has always given me
my color: big eyes, long nose,
reading too many books.

◊

Chromium ions are sensitive to their
chemical environment.
They make the ruby red,
the emerald green.

The ruby and emerald are similar.
You say red, I say green.

◊

An unattached electron
gives rise to color.
So can the absence of one of a pair
—a "color center."

Better to see oneself as
an unattached body
than half of a broken pair.

◊

The glass of some old bottles
contained iron and manganese.
Years of sunlight caused color centers,
the bottles became desert-amethyst glass.

But excessive heat
can destroy the color center,
and the color.
A hot amethyst turns citrine quartz,
or the rare greened quartz.

The heat of contained anger
can destroy a woman's center.
She appears ordinary
until it is released.

◊

In semiconductors
the band of energy levels
is split in two.
Between the band of lower energy levels
and the band of the more excited,
is the gap of forbidden energies.

My anger is forbidden energy.
The largest gap between
what I feel and what I say
renders me colorless.

◊

When wavelengths interfere
some amplify each other, others
cancel each other out.
The swirl of oil on water,
the gleaming beetle.

Our pasts interfere.
When hurt, we amplify our pain
and cancel each other out.
Yet we stay for the warmth,
the background gleam of joy.

◊

In a diffractive grating,
light is reflected from
equally spaced points or lines.
The light is scattered,
and waves from the openings interfere.
My mother's opal is a grating.
She loved it before it was understood.

The Evolution of Color Names

In the simplest languages,
all things are dark or light.

Red is always the first color
to be named after black and white.

Like fish dog chimp,
in sequence follow green and yellow,
blue brown purple,
pink orange gray.

Speakers of few color names
see as many colors
as any lexicographer.

To evoke a color,
they recall the world.

One African tongue
has no green, but
"water of sweet potato leaves."

Colorblind

The automobile accident
left the painter in a black and white world.
Years of colored abstracts
hung incoherent on studio walls.

To convey his new world,
he painted studio and furniture a range of grays
and set out a meal, also gray.
Only visitors escaped his gray brush.

His wife's "rat-colored" flesh repulsed him.
Unable to eat black tomatoes and gray meat,
he lived on Greek olives,
plain yogurt, and rice.

To survive without color,
he learned to inhabit the dark.

A nighthawk now,
he rises hours before dawn
to draw and sculpt

and drive to distant cities,
where he explores unfamiliar streets
and frequents all-night diners.

Phantom Light

Enucleation—the surgeon removes
a useless and dangerous eye.
In days before anesthesia,
at the moment when the scapel
severed the optic nerve,
the patient had a sensation of
light, not pain—
a single, gratuitous flash
that only confirmed the dark.

III

Everything Moves

Every liquid,
from tea to honey,
must flow—
and resist flowing.

A solid has an elastic limit.
Between that limit
and its breaking point,
carefully applied pressure
will make it move.

China mug with
Blue Willow pattern:

three men on a bridge,
water below;
tea swaying
as you carry it across the room.

A Stable Structure

constantly creates itself,
meets the same forces
with the same winning strategy;

as nightly adjustments
to thermostat and radio dial
deflect a spouse's anger,

and a body expands to breathe
beneath the weight
of another's sleeping arm.

A stable structure
is constantly tested.

A Diamond Is Hard But Not Tough

Tough material bends
to absorb a force.
By the time one breaks,
the pieces forget
their original shape.
The bent nail, the key
jammed in the lock.

In a hard material,
the first crack spreads so fast
a window appears to shatter
in an instant.
But the cracks run
clean through—
had they the patience, they
could have made Humpty ovoid again.

Under enough stress,
every material will fail.
If it cracks first, it's hard;
yields first, it's tough.
Both forms of failure
are potential in all things.

Structures

If a structure will stand for five minutes,
it will stand for five hundred years.
Prof. Jacques Heyman

Can I love you for five days,
five years, and then stop?

◊

The purpose of structure is delay.
Eventually, the weight falls,
strain is released.
Years, decades, centuries later
the event occurs.

Unable to resist
what is stronger than
any arrangement of parts,

a structure transmits forces—
the weight of a chair on the floor,
wind against the gate.

◊

A load abruptly applied
is more dangerous
than slowly accumulating
snow on a roof.

The most dangerous load
is slow but rhythmic.
Unnoticed, it grows in time—
soldiers marching on a footbridge.

◊

Paths of stress
around a small crack or nick
render the whole vulnerable—
the worn bedsheet
ripped at the edge.

Scored cardboard
is easy to bend.

Repairs that stiffen the old
add stress—the patched sleeve
that splits when the arm bends.

◊

Elastic materials
spring rapidly back to shape—
and springing back,
leave no record of strain.

Plastic materials
remain deformed:
small changes warn
that the breaking point nears.

◊

A taut string
is sensitive to change in stress.
A violinist turns the pegs
in tiny increments.
A Roman officer needed
a good musical ear
to adjust the catapult ropes.

◊

Placing block upon block,
a child constructs a wall.

Mortar is not a glue
(friction alone
would keep bricks from sliding).

As rust expands,
like glue, it transmits shear.
A riveted joint improves with age.

◊

A tightly inserted nail
barely weakens wood—
unlike the hole
when the nail is removed.

A useless nail
is better left in place,
its head filed flat.

◊

The keystone of an arch
is no stronger or more important
than any other stone.
Each is key and
locks the others in place.

CODA

By the time they are built,
most structures end up heavier
than their designer intended.

Ancient Physics

Each body, said Aristotle,
tends to go to its preferred position.
In natural motion, a body moves to get there.
Violent motion is caused by an agent
(an arrow is shot into the air).

It was violent motion
that summer day in Philadelphia
when I was eleven or twelve. My father was
trimming the edges of the lawn, where
the grass fringed out over the walk, the walk
that later cracked and was repaved.

He must have been kneeling, something
he could hardly do now, an old man who walks
several miles a day for his heart, but whose
joints are stiff. Kneeling or sitting;
and I—I don't remember—
could have been in any position.

Why was I there? Was I on my way into
or out of the house? Delivering a message
from my mother? I have forgotten
so much—whether we spoke, argued,
or divided the lawn with our silence.

I don't even recall a raised arm,
a slight shift of the torso, before
the violent motion of the gardening shears
heading—such a short distance—
through the air towards me.

They landed in the ground not far from me.
I do remember—perhaps memory exaggerates—
the shears, point down, quivering.
And then the natural motion of my body
entering the house, going to my room.

Torque

is the product of
the magnitude of the force
and the perpendicular distance
to the pivot point

(how hard you turn
what size wrench).

In other words, if I consider
this stone of pain in me the pivot point
and you the force,

the greater distance between us,
the harder I spin.

Knot Theory

A closed loop of
one-dimensional string
winds through
three-dimensional space.

The fundamental problem
is how to tell
one knot from another.

Size and shape don't matter—
only the arrangement of crossings,
over and under.

No essential information is lost
if you extract the knot
and study the space around it.

Though the shape of the space
I currently occupy
differs from shapes of the past,

an examination of
the tangled loops and whorls
would reveal persistent forms.

The Cat in the Box

A cat is placed in a box.
Inside, a device can release a fatal gas.
A random atomic event
will determine
if the gas is released.

The box is closed.
A moment later, the gas
has been either released or not released.

    Acrid with fear and sweat,
    the people are jostled, prodded,
    herded to the showers, handed towel and soap.
    The door clanks shut, a technician
    moves the lever.

According to classical physics,
the cat is either dead or not dead.
According to my mother, my dentist,
to common sense.

    The people lie piled atop one another,
    limp on the concrete floor.
    Unless the plumbing failed; in which case,
    they still await the water's stream.

Most quantum mechanicians say
the hidden cat lies in
a netherland between the two possibilities
and the actualization of one.
Only when someone lifts the lid to look inside
does one possibility vanish.
Only then is the cat dead or alive.

If the guard is particularly meticulous
in how he lines up the next bunch,
those inside may hover longer, cloth
in hand, awaiting the steely gaze
to release them into death.

Those physicists who subscribe to
the Many Worlds Interpretation
claim that when the experiment begins,
the world splits into two,
each with a cat in a box.
The worker who peeks into the box
becomes two, each oblivious of the other.
One self sees a dead cat,
the other a live cat.

As in another world,
the guard opens the door to find
people impatient to wash. Perhaps a few
even dancing, joyful with the knowledge
of what they missed.

Time Dilation

Einstein said that
the astronaut traveling through space
at close to the speed of light
ages more slowly
than one left behind.

My sister, launched by death
into the thin air of memory,
has aged hardly at all.
She is still in her twenties,
certain that her life
will be filled with music.

Earthbound, I became
bound to the past,
when we wore matching watches;
afraid to change
beyond all recognition.

Quantum Theory

The casket
they flew across the continent
stood cold and secretive,
sealed shut.

No one at the funeral
jumped up screaming and lifted the lid.
Our eyes could not pierce
its synthetic exterior.

We floated on waves of shock
and grief. Nightmarish possibilities
flashed in our minds, crumbled,
reappeared.

But we never made
the measurement of her death—
no one who loved her
saw her dead.

Fuse

A fuse blows.

Darkness but no danger.
Silence, shouts of surprise;
an iron unplugged, a switch reset.

Lights go on, music resumes.
Time circles again
on the now misleading clock.

The beauty of the fuse
is one of pure limit—
an intentional weak link

poised to break the circuit
before it can fail into fire.

Fire Safety

Forget the extinguishers,
the response time of engines and firefighters
measured in minutes.
When people die, it is for lack of escape.

No building is fireproof, no haven danger-free.
But with alternate routes,
if the first feels hot,
there's at least one other way out.

In a Taxco hotel, fire instructions,
in Spanish and English,
ended with advice to stay calm:

Ya que más que el incendio,
se puede morir por pánico.
Remember, aside from the fire you can die of panic.

IV

Asymmetry

The starry flounder
hatches symmetrical from the egg.

When the larva's a quarter inch long,
one eye begins   drifting
                                        toward the top of the skull.

From the other side (the fish is transparent)
you could watch the migrating eye.

Five days later, the adult fish
lies on the sea floor:
                                        both eyes looking up.

Sea Anemone

Eerily vivid
as an O'Keeffe flower,
color perpetually
washed by salt water,

the sea anemone
silently waves its delicate fringe.

The faceless, sightless
jewel-hued polyp
gracefully coaxes prey
into its hollow self.

The stubby cylindrical gut
gorges beyond capacity, holds
excess catch for hours

only to release it undigested,
unharmed.

When the greedy beauty
desires to move,
it lets go, floats away

and reattaches itself
wherever it falls.

The Mudskipper

In mangrove swamps
evolved a homely fish
with closely set,
protruding eyes.

Predator of small crabs,
bugs and snails,
the froglike fish

scoots across the mud,
propelled, as on crutches,
by stubby forefins.

Alarmed, it leaps off
in yard-long bounds;
or climbs a tree
with suckerlike pelvic fins.

The fish emerges
from water,
gill chambers filled
with a mixture of water and air.

It hunts, frolics,
and mates on land,
yet can survive indefinitely

under water,
breathing through its gills
like an ordinary fish.

Berry

From a shrub called
Synsepalum dulciferum
West Africans pick
the small red berries.

Chew a single berry
and for hours after
everything sour
tastes sweet.

Follow the Leader

At night the processionary caterpillars
stream down from their tree-hung nests
looking for food.

Relying on touch, they march head-to-tail
in a column many yards long.
If the chain is broken,
those ahead wait for the gap to close.

As each spins a tiny silk strand
the path beneath them
thickens.

Work done,
they return to their nests
guided by the sticky trail.

If the leader is made
to loop back to the end,
the rest will follow
in a circle that keeps on turning.

Only cold alters the scene.
At night they crawl to the center
to heap together for warmth

then at dawn
return along the silken spokes
to their places on the wheel.

Eventually hunger drives
a new leader astray

or the turning
slackens
as they
slowly
starve
to death.

Abscission, Leave-taking

With the first autumn chill
each leaf sends its food
back to the tree

as one about to die
prepares her possessions
for those she will leave behind.

Colors veiled by
summer's green
appear—
the old lady
flaunts her feverish beauty

until the world loosens its hold

and her own slight weight
is enough
to release her
through the air.

Fossils

Unlucky in life perhaps, yet
lucky (for us) in death. Buried quickly,
then left in peace
for the delicate process of hardening.

Holders of memories for other minds,
plants and creatures of small or no minds—

in their long deaths,
detailed in stone,
they tell far more than they knew.

V

Alberobello, First Carnival Night

Wooden stands, raised
with the swiftness of pop-up
castles in a children's book,

display stiff leather shoes,
bright scarves, and plaster models
of the church at the end of the street.

At the other end is the town square,

and a thirty-foot-high bandstand white
and lacy as a caliope, its entire crown
embroidered with multi-colored lights.

An old man still adds bulbs and wiring,

while three men with a ladder
make their way slowly up the street
between square and church.

At each post they stop. Two men
hold the ladder, while the other climbs
and places another light.

At Lunchtime

An elderly couple sit
in a coffeeshop booth.
His button says:
I am Blind and Deaf.

When he signs, she
reaches to reply, and
their hands move
like grounded birds.

Their periods of silence
are no longer
than ours when we eat together.

Done, she rises first.
He takes her arm as she
motions for the check,
a smile on her patient face.

At the register
his hand seeks out her shoulder,
then goes to her neck
where it nestles firmly.

Giacometti

Giacometti once told me that he tried to depict the world as it would appear in a purely visual way, say to someone who had been born without hands, who had no sense of touch.

Arthur Danto

The artist of touch
coaxes and bruises his figures
into their lonely quest,
to lean into a place
where a man is sculptural
only in the sense of present—
a pulse, a posture.
This thin essence, a narrow
cold bronze flame,
rends the fabric of space before one's eyes.
There is no need to touch
such a one, no responding desire
to be touched. Just
the recognition that you, too,
could be pared down to this.

The Exhibition

Each painting,
with watchmaker precision
and Flemish attention to light,
lovingly presents
a glorious human mess.

The strokes of oil
dwell on the still warm curves of
unmade beds, crumpled cigarette packs,
piles of newspapers in every room,
edges hanging over,
milk left in glasses, glasses left on tables,
matchbooks, pillows, ticket stubs, letters,
papers on the floor, on the radiator,
under a pile of clothes.

I stand in the bare gallery
peering into the giant canvases,
crawling into the beds,
adding my clothes to a pile,
leaving an unanswered letter on the sill.

Snow

Maps simplify the world somewhat in the way a heavy snowfall does...
Robert Harbison, *Eccentric Spaces*

A Leonard Bernstein young people's concert on TV.
On the other side of the picture window, snow fell
heavily; quietly but not truly silently; blanketing
but not truly covering
the usual dissonances, the overly rehearsed routines.

Our parents were on their way to New York. We stayed
home, old enough to want Lenny and music, to sense
the magic of an hour when white maps the familiar,
leaving it strange, when snow is unsullied, and
clarity is not grasped but only treasured.

Sister

In the living room,
modern furniture and no mess,
father paced and mumbled
his accompaniment to mother's days
calibrated into endless minor tasks.

Days punctuated by his temper
and capped by the tension at dinner.
Starved for clues, we grew to hate their
secrecy about everything—
from money to how they cast their vote.

At night when they were in bed,
we held private tea parties, with Nabisco
cookies fanned out on a plate.
Bemoaning their shrunken lives,
we speculated on buried tragedies.

Now that you are gone,
we have our tragedy.
His steps are slower, her tasks fewer.
While I sit alone with my cookies and tea,
determined to crack the code.

In the Afternoon

My hip aches from the damp
and I dream
of afternoons in Paris
where even rainy days are light.

A scene in the novel
describes a clocharde and the narrator
drinking wine together on a smelly
curb.
She hospitably unbuttons him, and
works him with her
vari-stained hands and tongue.
My own mounting breath
surprises me.

The rain brings night even
closer. One bulb left in the high-ceilinged
room.
The ladder is locked away by
the superintendent, who asked to see
my poems
while brushing my breast with his hand—
that was the last time he'll take
me by surprise.

The phone rings. I refuse to
answer,
to let my mother's questions enter
the dark room of my book,
bring muggers into its gardens,
or interrupt the rain.

Map of My Father's Death

The last roads he walked are pale: here legs
and mind faltered. In these buildings, they tried
to bolster a body winding down, then advised
a lowering of expectations—rising from the couch
slowly, patience with fumbling for keys. Cities
and towns have misspelled names. Foliage is
faint, the coastline blurred. This is the road
where his decline hastened. With few turns and no
intersections, it goes clear to the edge of the page.

Norma

I

Night comes, snow falls. In this city,
it is hard for a solitary person
to prepare a warm evening.
Outside, flakes will
melt on my face.
You are too distant now
to come down with the snow; to return
wet or cold, or with any shape.
A friend wrote a poem
about your slender wrists,
just after Grandpa died.

Your wrists and snow—
both tiny, both gone quickly
just as the loveliness brightens.

II

Yesterday the silken lavender clouds
drove me crazy with dismay.
So beautiful.

You say, "Let me share
those clouds with you.
If you couple me only with
rotted leaves after rain and
the mangled bodies of small animals,
you will refuse
the only gift I can give you.
If I am no more than your largest loss,
your standard will be loss. Whatever
hurts the most you will
honor the most, call life."

III

Tonight I talked with mother.
I said your name, Norma, like
a plain word
that describes something solid and visible,
an apple of Cezanne's. Glowing,
with a presence more than apple—
on fire,
timeless, all that—
apple apple apple
Norma Norma Norma
I said your name.

She asked did I want
a certain book of guitar songs
(she'd made a list).
I said, "That one must have been Norma's."
She did not banish me from her garden.
I was a follower in exile,
obedient without a home.
I knocked at the gate,
then broke her law.
I said your round red name,
oh, Norma.

About the Author

Photo by Walter Crump

Ann Rae Jonas was born in New York City. After graduating from Goddard College she worked as a printer, drafter, waiter, and ghostwriter. Since receiving her M.A. in science writing from Johns Hopkins University, she has been the editor of *StarDate* magazine and an editor at the Minnesota Geological Survey; currently she is the Catalog Manager at The MIT Press. She is the author of the *Museum of Science Book of Answers & Questions.* Her poetry has appeared in such journals as *Frank, River City, Artful Dodge,* and *Seneca Review.*

About the Artist

In 1988, Randy Jewart began stone carving at William & Mary when he was a student there majoring in English and Education. Randy's figurative imagery comes from the relationship between a feeling or idea and how it manifests itself as gesture. He has shown in numerous national juried exhibitions in Columbus, OH; Cooperstown, NY; Loveland, CO; New Castle, PA; and Helena, MT.

A Diamond Is Hard But Not Tough is the winner of the 1997 Word Works Washington Prize. Ann Rae Jonas's manuscript was selected from 400 manuscripts submitted by American poets.

FIRST READERS:

Jane Alberdeston
Nancy Allinson
Jamie Brown
William Derge
Pat Gray
James Hopkins
Tod Ibrahim
Hiram Larew
Sydney March
Steven B. Rogers
Jonathan Vaile
Marcella Wolfe

SECOND READERS:

Miles David Moore
Sharon Negri
Robert Sargent

FINAL JUDGES:

Martha Sanchez-Lowery, Director
Donald Cunningham, Co-Director
Karren L. Alenier
J.H. Beall
Hilary Tham

About the Word Works

The Word Works, a nonprofit literary organization, publishes contemporary poetry in collector's editions. Since 1981, the organization has sponsored the Washington Prize, an award of $1,000 to a living American poet. Each summer, Word Works presents free poetry programs at the Joaquin Miller Cabin in Washington, DC's Rock Creek Park. Annually, two high school students debut at the Miller Cabin Series as winners of the Young Poets Competition.

Since Word Works was founded in 1974, programs have included: "In the Shadow of the Capitol," a symposium and archival project on the African-American intellectual community in segregated Washington, DC; the Gunston Arts Center Poetry Series (including Ai, Carolyn Forché, Stanley Kunitz, Linda Pastan, among others); the Poet-Editor panel discussions at the Bethesda Writer's Center (including John Hollander, Maurice English, Anthony Hecht, Josephine Jacobsen, among others); Poet's Jam, a multi-arts program series featuring poetry in performance; a poetry workshop at the Center for Creative Non-Violence (CCNV) shelter, and the Writers' Retreat workshops and readings in Tuscany. In 1997 the Word Works began distributing chapbooks by Mica Press (Ft. Collins, Colorado) under a cooperative agreement.

Past grants have been awarded by the National Endowment for the Arts, the National Endowment for the Humanities, the DC Commission on the Arts and Humanities, the Witter Bynner Foundation, and others, including many generous private patrons.

Word Works has an archive of artistic and administrative materials in the Washington Writing Archive housed in the George Washington University Gelman Library.

Please enclose a self-addressed stamped envelope with all inquiries. Find out more about the Word Works at
http://www.writer.org/wordwork/wordwrk1.htm

Other available Word Works books:

Karren L. Alenier, **Wandering on the Outside**
J. H. Beall, **Hickey, The Days...**
John Bradley, **Love-In-Idleness***
Grace Cavalieri, **Pinecrest Resthaven,** *(Capital Collection)*
Shirley Cochrane, **Family and Other Strangers**
Harrison Fisher, **Curtains for You**
Barbara Goldberg, **Berta Broadfoot and Pepin the Short**
Linda Lee Harper, **Toward Desire***
James McEuen, **Snake Country,** *(Capital Collection)*
Elaine Magarrell, **Blameless Lives***
Fred Marchant, **Tipping Point***
Barbara Moore, **Farewell to the Body***
Miles David Moore, **The Bears of Paris,** *(Capital Collection)*
Jay Rogoff, **The Cutoff***
Robert Sargent, **Aspects of a Southern Story**
Robert Sargent, **Woman From Memphis**
M.A. Schaffner, **The Good Opinion of Squirrels,** *(Capital Collection)*
Enid Shomer, **Stalking the Florida Panther***
Hilary Tham, **Bad Names for Women,** *(Capital Collection)*
Nancy White, **Sun, Moon, Salt***
George Young, **Spinoza's Mouse***

**Washington Prize winners*

Karren L. Alenier, *ed.,* **Whose Woods These Are**

Christopher Bursk, *ed.,* **Cool Fire** *(A chapbook from the Creative Center for Non-Violence workshop)*

Moshe Dor, Barbara Goldberg, and Giora Leshem, *eds.* **The Stones Remember**

Betty Parry, *ed.,* **The Unicorn and the Garden**

Issac Goldberg, **Solomon Ibn Gabirol: A Bibliography of his Poems in Translation**

Requests for our brochure and other information must be accompanied by a self-addressed stamped envelope.